Monty Grows New Clothes

by
Margaret Woodhouse

MONTY GROWS NEW CLOTHES
Text and illustrations copyright © Margaret Woodhouse 1990

All rights reserved.
No part of this book may be reproduced in any form.

First published 1990

LDA
Duke Street, Wisbech, Cambs. PE13 2AE

LD 961
ISBN 1-85503-088-8 Paperback
ISBN 1-85503-095-0 Hardback

Created and designed by Magari Publishing, PO Box 74 266, Auckland New Zealand.
Printed and bound in New Zealand by Interprint Printing.

Monty Monarch's mother was a gorgeous creature.

She had lovely orange and brown wings which she fluttered as she passed. And their edges were trimmed in black and white, just like fur.

She was such a social butterfly, you would know her anywhere. And she brushed against the snapdragons and drank nectar from the roses.

She met Monty's father in the buttercup meadow. They whispered in the wind and together they made Monty and all his brothers and sisters.

When it was time for Monty to be born, his mother laid him as an egg on a milkweed leaf. Then she darted off again to dip and dive in the sun, leaving Monty to fend for himself.

Monty hatched six days later. He didn't look at all like his mother. In fact, you would hardly think them related. He came out of the egg long and stripy, gold and black ...... and very hungry.

Now, Monty was not at all keen on spinach, and he didn't think much of pumpkin, but he was very partial to milkweed leaves. So his mother had left him in just the right spot.

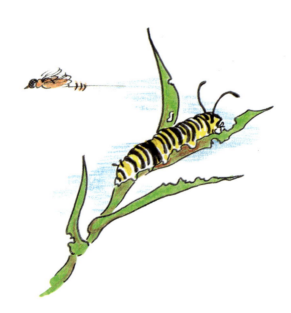

In no time at all he was feeding on the milkweed plant.

For two whole weeks he chomped and swallowed. So large did he grow that he had to change his stripy suit FOUR times. Yet he kept on eating the delicious leaves.

One day, however, he began to get restless. He wiggled up a branch and began to weave a thick thread of silk under the shelter of a twig. With a sudden shuffle and a wobble he grabbed the thread and threw off his last set of striped clothes.

There, underneath, was Monty the chrysalis.

How handsome he looked under his blue-green cloak. It was studded with little spots of gold, making him look like a jewel that his mother might wear around her neck.

Monty swung in the breeze and sparkled and shone. For two weeks he was hanging about like this. And during that time the little gold spots were helping to colour the wings that Monty was growing under his chrysalis skin.

Slowly Monty's whole colour and shape changed. When the two weeks had passed his cloak began to crack and one light, warm day a new Monty appeared.

He was wet and floppy when he first emerged.

But once he had dried himself in the sun he looked splendid! He had orange and brown wings and their edges were trimmed in black and white, just like fur!

Now it was Monty's turn to swirl in the wind. He soon learned to dance about the flowers and drink from their petals. Through the long Summer days he got to know the other Monarch Butterflies in his

neighbourhood and he flirted with all the girls.

He became such a social butterfly - you would know him anywhere.

By the time Winter came Monty needed to rest. He followed the others over the hills to a warm, sheltered spot where he would be safe from the frosts. All the other butterflies crowded around him and as far as the eye could see they slept in a carpet of orange and brown, black and white.

Monty felt happy there. And he nestled in, in his lovely new clothes, to wait until he would be able to fly once more in the warm air of Spring.